DESECRATIONS

FROM DANTE'S *INFERNO*, CANTO I, LINES 1–18

In the milieu of middle age, life left-
Turned me to a wooded maze and the good
Old way forward went AWOL, 404, MIA.

Ah hell, it's tough to say what was what
In those savage, chiaroscuro trees:
So bitter-cold a coffin sounded cozy.

Just speaking of it now gives me the willies!
But all that goes-with-grace, believe me,
Comes that way, so I say what I have to say.

Can't point to the place where I near kipped
In those nasty sticks: I was bushed,
Blotto, ready to rack out when I strayed.

I hit bottom at the bottom of a steep hill
That lifted then skirted the valley
Where all my fear and doubt came to play—

Vested and invested with that celestial light
We know shows men the sure road,
The ridge was dressed in fiery clothes.

DESECRATIONS

POEMS

MATT RADER

McClelland & Stewart

Library and Archives Canada Cataloguing in Publication

Rader, Matt, 1978-, author
    Desecrations / Matt Rader.

Poems.
Issued in print and electronic formats.
ISBN 978-0-7710-7248-2 (paperback). – ISBN 978-0-7710-7249-9 (epub)

    I. Title.

PS8585.A2825D48 2016   C811'.6   C2015-907721-4
                                               C2015-907722-2

Published simultaneously in the United States of America by McClelland & Stewart, a division of Random House of Canada Limited

Library of Congress Control Number is available upon request

Typeset in SabonNext by M&S, Toronto
Printed and bound in the USA

McClelland & Stewart,
a division of Random House of Canada Limited,
a Penguin Random House Company
www.penguinrandomhouse.ca

1   2   3   4   5   20   19   18   17   16

 Penguin
Random
House

For my friends and family,

This copper-pink feather of fern,
Japanese Autumn, autochthon of East Asia,
At home now on my island of origin—

CONTENTS

I shall create! If not a note, a hole.
If not an overture, a desecration.

GWENDOLYN BROOKS

I am a Hittite in love with a horse.

FRANK O'HARA

DESECRATIONS

WINTER HORSES
for Raph Assaf

A horse has a memory so perfect it can sleep
Standing up and begin to forget the world,
Moment by moment, in a starless pasture.
I have reached now, if I'm lucky or average,
The end of the first half of my life and I know
Very little of horses. One night, before I remember,
My father came home in a flood of headlights
So badly beaten my mother didn't recognize
The man staggering through the brightness.
There was no horse then like the dapple grey
I met last winter in the northern Rockies
Who didn't care about me or the late snow
Or the electric fence that had failed to cordon
Its allotment of darkness. That grey was
Complete in the sweep of lantern light:
Finite, ambivalent, the colour of winter skies.
The man who beat my father was his friend
And when my father called down Martin's wife
In the bar that night, Martin asked him to
Apologize like a friend and how many
Friends does a man really have? I see now
Two colossal dray horses, heads bowed in a field
Of shadows, their white mukluks of hair,
Their anoraks of muscle. The car turns
In the yard and the headlights scan the cabin,
Then my mother's twilit eyes, the black trees,
The road, the open field, the pair of high withers.

LEENANE, CONNEMARA, CO. GALWAY, IRELAND

All the mares are in love and the geldings
—Owens Eagle, Outta Touch, Young Grace—
Broken and haltered at the Clifden pony market.
At Rosro, at the mouth of Killary Harbour,
World War Two is finally over and daily
Wittgenstein eats mussels in melted butter.
"Seems before me only a long stretch of living
Death," he said once in a different context.
Meaning out of time. Unbounded present. Today
The blue dinghy in the tidal mud below Mweelrea
Is a shibboleth for something stuck or waiting
Or already on its way. So what kind of people
Do I really want to be? When will the tide
Be back in Leenane or Kinsale or Ballyhack?

HOMER
for Evie Christie

When you warned me not to rouse the hen
And peepers squatting on your balcony
I didn't dare mention Hector, Homer's pigeon,
Flapping wildly beneath the walls of Troy
As he and Achilles, in full flight,
Raced past the lookout and the fig tree
And the springs of Xanthos
Where before the war, wives and daughters
Scrubbed wedding blood
From chamber clothes in tubs of steam and snow water.
Four times, huffing, fucked,
Heartsick for the fight,
The homer and the hawk circled the city
Before Zeus finally tipped the scales on the two psychos.

CHOCOLATEY VERSUS ANNE DEVLIN

Maser's cameo-collection wall-art Anne Devlin
On the corner of Carmens Hall and Meath Street,
The Liberties, Dublin, versus Cadbury's white
Script *Chocolatey* on irradiated blue panelling.

Her Pantone 292 skin. Her card-white hair.
The Warhol-hued shawl we might call KSU™
Bleeding into Eminence™. That yolk-toned
Crème Egg–shaped stencil sprayed on concrete

Side by each with the corporate giddy-up to shift
From noun to adjective. Where modifier is what
The modified meant. A billboard in a compliment-
Ary hue we'd eyeball to be Reflex Blue™.

Who cares if we know who Anne Devlin is
Or where the tributaries of the River Poddle went
Or why *Houdini Bang Bang* is carved into the steps
Of the Coombe Lying-in-Hospital monument.

In Dean Swift's day these streets were bathed in night
Soil and Dutch Billys. Where Huguenots wove
Calimancoes, druggets, poplins shot with clock
Reel, culgy handkerchiefs. Where the weavers

Left off to cross the Liffey and be butchered
By the butchers of Ormond Quay. My mother's
Mother's mother likely lived here, scullery maid,
In the family way, at the turn of the 20th century.

4

It's 1803. Robert Emmet is hanged, drawn, and
Quartered on Thomas Street, and Devlin strung up
By the yeomanry on the very cart her father
Donated to midwife the aborted state. See Wikipedia

For further details and inaccuracies. Maser's
Liberties Festival pop-graph portrait head-to-head
With a miniature Devlin sat for at Rogerson's Quay
Two hundred years earlier. Which shows more

Torture in the rendered care of Edward Trevor,
Failed apothecary, Chief Medical Inspector,
Kilmainham Gaol? More damp straw and effluent? More
Erysipelas? Such tender mercy. Give us a sign.

MAVIS GALLANT
for Elizabeth Bachinsky, with a line from Maggie Nelson

All our poems now are for people we know
And our babies. It's 1846. In the North
Charitable Infirmary the musical society plays
The Bells of Shandon for the women of Cork
Who are so hungry their bellies recall
Those late days of pregnancy. "Men bores me,
Especially Great Men," is what I wish
I'd said to a woman I was trying to love once
With books and fucking. But all I know
About books and fucking is that they change
And I'm tired of men going on about men.
If loneliness is solitude with a problem.
If I'm scared alonely. What did they do
With all those babies and people we knew?

HIGHTOWN, CORALSTOWN, MULLINGAR, CO. WESTMEATH, IRELAND

for John Ennis

My first day in Hightown we called on the fields
Where your people seeded and reseeded the grass
For centuries: the forge field where your boy
Hopes to build a new home, where horse teams
Were hayed and reshod on the highway between
Dublin and Galway; the hurling field or field
For dancing where the long-bearded pipers played
In the evening with the fiddler down the boreen;
And the Lone Bush field where you've asked
Your children to leave your remains with the un-
Named babies beneath the thorn—the stillborns,
Aborts, unbaptized—where your man from Aran
Blessed the unmarked graves, where your father
Staggered one night and returned, unable to speak.

My Life Aboard the Last Sailing Ship
Carrying Cumberland Coal

You give your first-born daughter
A central-Asian name
Meaning blue or water.
Years later two bluebirds alight on either arm
And an artist's quick needlework
Stitches birds to skin
So even
In your obsequies your fetlocks
Wing away, appear then disappear. Of course
Now you are a horse

With pale blue withers on a high Afghan plain.
What does it mean to be
Such a thing? Behind you, the blue Pamir mountains.
Before you, antiquity.
You follow a trade in lapis lazuli
From Badakhshan to the court of Cleopatra.
You see morning's blue aurora
Alight on the Nile Delta and around the eyes
Of the pharaoh. Oh.
Oh,

Isis, God of sailors. Entering the Salish Sea
Pamir becalms in a thick mist
Off Cape Flattery.
The water beneath the ship is dark lapis.
You are on the yard of the crossjack working canvas.
Out of the blue
The blue
Wings of eros and agape alight in you. Deus ex caritas.
Your God is born.
Cape Horn.

Galapagos. Azores.
The hurricane with a woman's name that sinks *Pamir*
Off the blue shores
Of the Portuguese vernacular.
It all comes together in the English word
Azure. The hue of your daughter's eyes.
Cognate of lapis lazuli.
The bird
A sailor gets on his arm for sailing the globe in three thousand years.
The horse that gathers away, appears then disappears.

PERVERTS
for Michael V. Smith

It's one of those things in geology. We get
A glimpse into a moment far far back
In misery. Let's go deeper into that moment.
Between the flowering of the lotus
And the flowering of the water lily,
Between White Sands Proving Ground
And the basalt flows of Imnaha, Oregon,
Between finance and poetry, comes
A love that's kind and patient and injures
All things. That's a lotus you see flowering
On the left. That's a water lily flowering
On the right. We've talked so often
Of fathers we're bored deadly. After
White Bird died and Looking Glass died,
And Time died as he had known it,
On October 5, 1877, Chief Joseph
Conceded to General Nelson Appleton Miles
In the Bears Paw Mountains. Not even
The mountains had always been mountains.

Talking Trojan War Blues

"All the new thinking is about death,"
Robert Hass said, longingly, in a scribble
Of blackberries. I was dreaming Seamus Heaney
On the porch while the children pedalled
Their bicycles down the street,
Dragging their long, late-summer shadows
To death behind them. Such tender
Desecration. Even Achilles' horses wept
In the field of battle days before
They were made to drag through dust
Hector's body. "Longing, we say,
Because desire is full of endless distances."
Robert Hass said that. You can be in my dream
If I could just remember it. I said that.

CORMAC'S, MANORHAMILTON, CO. LEITRIM, IRELAND

Someone has disappeared the famine
Graves from the village map and the work-
House is full of empty windows. In Cormac's
The boys are at home with themselves
Along the bar. "They were old comrades,"
Yeats wrote of Hamilton's men, "and knew
Each other's lives," and as they rode
Through birch boughs and quicken trees,
The gloaming clotting the clouds
Above Ben Bulben and Cashel-na-Gael,
They recited their wounds like names
Of children, fathers, women. No one
Sits alone at Cormac's bar and no one eats
And no one speaks of Stranger's Leap.

Everything You Wanted to Know About the Dead But Were Afraid to Ask the Ice-Fishers at Gardom Lake

The ice-fishers gather around their good friend
As he augers a hole in the ice. In the deep
Unconscious of the lake mud, turtles and frogs
Are neither alive nor dead. Here come the women
Across the lens of the lake with milk and honey,
The black ewe's blood. They pour it in the fresh pupil
And disturb the cloudy ghosts in the black water.
The dead are cold and haggard. Bless their hearts.
The rainbow trout are neither alive nor dead.
The eastern brook trout are neither alive nor dead.
They are the silver dynamism in the blind depth.
Like the dead they come to us on their own time.
The ice-fishers settle down in their folding chairs
Under the sun, beyond the Groves of Persephone.

A common year beginning in my memory.
By March, in dark pools beneath Lake Erie
And in the zinc mines of Kamioka Mining
& Smelting Company, Gifu Prefecture,
Neutrinos from a collapsing supergiant
On the outskirts of a nearby dwarf galaxy,
Caromed through sensitive, hyper-pure water.
I was eight years old. For the first time
In nearly four hundred years a supernova
Was visible to the naked eye from Las
Campanas Observatory, Chilean Andes,
To the Nōbi Plain, where the great sword-
Makers of the shogunates are remembered
And the clear river waters drawn for sake.
I was thirty-eight years old. That spring,
While night contracted to its most exquisite
Northern density, the decaying light grew
Brighter in its deep pool of space above
The Salish Sea and the Morton Salt girl,
In her short smock and yellow Mary Janes,
Who'd been walking that faded billboard
With her umbrella in the ever-sleet, outside
Fairport Harbor, Ohio, for so long she could no
Longer be seen by the commuters flowing
West along Route 2 to Cleveland.
I was sixty-eight years old. Then, in June,

After the persimmons bloomed in Gifu
And the Nagara River lipped its levies,
After doctors in Miami and New York City
First wrote scripts for low-dose AZT,
A drug that inhibits reverse transcription
And production of complementary DNA,
That crystallizes into a salt superstructure
As in the Morton mines below Lake Erie,
The light began to fade. I was ninety-eight.

LUNAR NEW YEAR'S DAY, YEAR OF THE SNAKE
for Eduardo C. Corral

The cross steepling St. George's is so empty.
Meanwhile, vultures cyclone
Their shadows motherfucking slowly.
Meanwhile, five bison
Skulls on the barn wall sport one
Or two small black annuities
Terminating where their brains
Would be.
Meanwhile, fingerprints, Charybdis, drains. Again,
All good fortune is wealth,
All ill fortune the ouroboros of luck feeding
Itself itself.
St. George's is so lonely evenings
After the Narcotics Anonymous meetings.

When For a Time I Loved Two Women

You lived as though no one knew your name.
Across the lake, hills hummed with wildfire
So at night a rash of red-orange eyes stared
Back across the surface, a tremble of beasts
Stamping and snorting through the whorl of ash—
Possessed, vatic—ready for you to disrobe
Before the cool, void slate of water.
Already the stars were redacted by smoke
While hikers and coyotes bellied down
In the creek to escape the black lace of flames.
On those nights, when you stood naked, alone
Or with company, at the edge of the lake,
Skin ringing through the dark city park,
You dragged laughter slowly across your face.

We lived as though jokes were overtures
Unexplained. It is better, we thought, to set
A sea-green Kraken of aloe in a window pot
Than keep a good journal. The rubber
Plant steered its fleshy paddles toward a shore
Made entirely of light and we noted this
Grace daily over plates of pork and rice.
Already we wore thin jackets to help us
Forgive the wind, while helicopters blew
Rain beads off acre on acre of dark cherries.
In those days, when spiders dressed the deck
In delicate knitwear the colour of water,
And all our friends drifted off in aeroplanes,
We'd not yet heard that one about birds.

I lived as though the weather had nothing
To do with me and the tired August light
Was never disappointed to be light and be tired.
I'd swim out in the river with one woman
And then another and by a wry wave of hands
We'd hang in the current and watch galaxies
Of dust swirl by on warped panes of water.
Already crickets were assembling evening
With its failing memory for faces and light
While clouds flowed like fire across the sky.
In those years, when I saw a woman's face,
Above or below me, eyes stricken, perfect,
Closing on something too bright or distant
For me to see, I understood little of the hilarity.

Everything About You Reminds Me of You
But It's Not My Name You Say in Your Sleep

After seven years of only half-reluctant lovemaking
In the caves of Ogygia, beyond bowers of cypress
And fields of flowering parsley, Calypso didn't know
How Odysseus felt until on the shore their last day
He returned her kiss before the gods and eternity.

And not until she'd held his wrist, then his hand
In her hand, then his fingers, then only his eyes
With her eyes, as the raft, cached with bread and wine,
Gathered on the waves, did Odysseus, who'd not
Seen his wife in decades, fear Calypso letting go.

Indigenous Cities

I wanted to show Annie a painting by Jack Yeats
At the Galway City Museum, but we arrived late
And tired to our hotel. A large Irish wedding reception
Occupied the ballroom and the lobby, a melee
Of jacketless men whose ties had come undone,
Women hooking their high heels in one hand, parents
Wrangling bleary, drunken children toward
The lift. By then, I had no heart for paintings.
It was mid-May and though the days were long
In the North Atlantic, it was dark and rainy
That evening. I'd always had a sense growing up
In Canada of May as like an eyeball, exposed,
An insomniac's eyeball, an eyeball open too long
To the light, but it's a simile I'd never cared to pursue.
When you drive north in the North during spring
And summer, you don't so much approach the sun
As move not so far away. In winter, when driving
North you can feel the curvature of Earth
As the sun's warmth weakens on your back.
I'd had the sense that evening leaving the Flaggy Shore
For Galway we were no longer so far away.
We'd had to stop for directions half a kilometre
South of University College Hospital. I asked a man
Who stood smoking in a doorway, a burnished gold
Chain connecting lapel to a pocket watch
In his breast pocket—this was the kind of anachronism
My mind was forever making note of in Ireland
Before being ratcheted into the symbolic code
Of watches, chains, history, the word *Khronos*
Clocked inside the lexicon of my own narrative

Observations, the idea of "wrong time." I told him
The name of the hotel we were looking for. "Fuck me,"
He said, "you've gotta go all the way back," then
Waved his hand, explaining it was five minutes north
Past the Hospital, the Uni, and the intersection
With the N6, all the way up to where Upper Newcastle
Becomes the N59 to Clifden. I forgot to ask the time.
We'd travelled north that morning from Miltown Malbay
Along the N67 to Lahinch then joined the R478,
Crossed the Inagh River and continued west
Through Liscannor before heading north again
Just prior to St. Brigid's Well and on then, finally,
To the Cliffs of Moher. We wanted to go walking
At the cliffs because everyone goes walking there
And we felt our own delights would be sharpened
By shared experience, by the uncommon common,
That rare in our lives that occupies the same rare
Place in the lives of others, allowing us to recognize
Ourselves as individuals who belong to a crowd
Of like and unlike individuals. Besides, we didn't
Want to miss out on an experience—or "experience"
As I had theorized in the grant proposal—that was
Sure to embody a Kantian sublime. It wasn't
An amusement park, after all, that had to be designed
And cast and riveted to the earth. It wasn't a work
Of art. It was a dramatic natural phenomenon
In a chain of geological deep time. Also, I wanted to read
Wallace Stevens's "The Irish Cliffs of Moher"
At the Cliffs of Moher and enter yet another pane
In the hall of mirrors. Annie was driving because
She'd lived in Japan with an Austrian chef named Josiah
And was therefore more accustomed to driving
On the left than I. She'd driven in Australia too,

Another place where passage was negotiated in the mirror
Of my habituation, making the 3,066-kilometre trek
From Melbourne to Cairns in a hired Toyota Land Cruiser
For no reason she'd share with me other than that
She'd wanted to "make some kind of journey" before
Returning to Japan where she worked for a multinational
Lawyering agency. (She did admit, once, while drinking
In Seattle, that she'd experienced "a pharmaceutical
Mix-up" in Melbourne that resulted in her snorting
Methamphetamine on the top of a toilet tank
On the last night of a strange conference of activists,
Lawyers, and artists. The conference had no clear purpose,
A kind of hurricane of intellectualism and sex that had at its eye
The idea of indigenous cities. "This," she'd said in Seattle,
In the midst of a different hurricane, "may have been
A factor." Indigeneity, at that point, was a subject
We kept on standby.) Yes, Annie was driving
Through the narrow roadway, and green, and wind-
Combed countryside of Co. Clare. All along the R478,
I watched small white farmhouses and gorse and fields
And paddocks of "tiny grasses dreaming," as I'd read
One evening on a mistranslated sign on the Internet.
"Let a hundred flowers bloom!" I'd said aloud to no one.
A small sign, not quite knee-high, the Chinese characters
Aligned above the English forming a title or epigraph
I assumed said "Keep Off" but to my Western mind
Had an aura that read "mystery." I'd thought
On that sign from time to time while looking at lawns
In Annie's Toronto, and in New York City
And in the Okanagan Valley, where I was attempting
To make a new life—and where, according to a colleague
At the university, over eighty species of grasses thrived.
Driving through western Ireland's tiny grasses

I thought again of how much poetry relied
On mistranslation, a love of the gaps, the fertile
Interstitial space between *meaning* and *mean*. Or,
Fuck me. The frisson of the possible, as they say,
When the ineffable becomes an utterance of the relentless
And discomfiting multiple. It is the kind of paradox
That poetry and poets love. Out the window the small
White farmhouses and gorse and fields traded places
With other small white farmhouses and gorse and fields
And it was beautiful like all patterns imbued with tiny,
Unpredictable variations. We parked in a large lot
Of rented cars and tour buses and paid our €6 each
And, wrapping our scarves around our pale necks
And pulling on our toques, crossed the two-lane highway
In the direction of the cliffs and all that wind
Evacuating the Atlantic in cold panic. We were tired
And in the middle of our day. The cliffs were a beacon,
A destination that stood in for all desires in our lives
That, at the time, were diffuse or amorphous.
It was a period we'd look back on as productive
Confusion for Annie and me both. We were talking about
Babies. I was still married. Annie's sister had just
Been released from prison after fourteen years.
We didn't, in those days, quite know what we wanted
To have happen in our lives or where we wanted to go.
Annie knew she wanted to make documentary films
About her family, who had been formed and un-
Formed by immigration, crime, and the steel factories
Of southern Ontario, but when her mind turned
To that history she was overwhelmed by a feeling
So powerful and grey, she told me, it would not permit
Being identified or outlined or given any relief or shape.
Framed in Annie's memory were several things

She said she couldn't imagine: her sister at twenty-one
Holding the grey baby on Annie's doorstep; or after,
Her sister at thirty-four, crossing the road toward
Her and her parents, having emerged from an office
Of empty, impenetrable windows only seconds
Prior, sporting black slacks and a grey sweater,
The embodied absence of family photos, the full void,
The *figura* around which Annie had arranged so
Much of her adult anxieties, her perception of space.
Her sister might have been leaving the accountant's.
For my part, I wanted to get away from my life
In Canada, to gain some purchase, some advantage—
To confuse a *figura etymologica*—on how I felt
And how I thought I was supposed to feel. I imagined
The elements of my life—my children, my wife,
My body—as thin, nearly two-dimensional
Panes of glass hung against gravity in something
Resembling a fully immersive digital space where
No edges obtained, no borders. When the panes
Were rearranged—when they found a particular
But unpredictable alignment—and I stood at a certain
Angle, I could see myself in a way that would
Make clear to me what I needed, what kind of person
I could stand to be. The Cliffs of Moher were a "Real"
We could see and touch and feel. It was the one place
We both knew we wanted to be. Annie was thin.
Her parents were thin and her aunt who worked
At Dunne's on St. Patrick and Bowling Green
In Cork City was thin. All those people lined up
There above the ocean, a slim projection, a hologram
Bearing those particular coordinates of history
In that moment in that place. I decided to take her
Picture. I clicked the exposure button and the shutter

Shuddered. I hoped the portrait of Annie would capture
Some of the phantasmagoria of the moment—
The swirling light, the soft-focus lichen splotching
The lookout's safety wall, Annie with her blue eyes,
Hair tucked up into her burnished-gold knitwear,
Her family flickering over her presence as if she were
Only an expression of light and RNA. I refused to check
The view-screen. I let the thing hang self-consciously
Over my shoulder. Small lines of tourists were arranged
Erratically in both directions along the narrow path
That skirted the lip of the cliffs. Flashes of light
Pinged off the overcast afternoon like Doppler
Readings reporting moments of human weather. Light
Was varnishing the cracked panels of sky above
The ocean, which added to the drama and the spooling
Exposition in my mind on cameras and the ethics
Of mediated reality, my own inner narration
That either separated or bound me to my surroundings,
Something I'd heard Robert Hass say in a poem
About another coast some 8,034 kilometres away.
A man in a green cap sat on a chair on the path
Playing a hand-pump harmonium like a dream
Of Wallace Stevens who had his own ideas of order
And his own beach in the Florida Keys. Annie
Gave the man money. Later, just north of O'Brien's
Tower, I got down on my belly and slid my body
Forward to regard the 702 feet between me
And the black rocks that jawed the surf like meat.
The painting I'd wanted to show Annie is called
Communicating with Prisoners and depicts
Mothers and sisters in their big winter coats
And hats, their scarves and shawls, heads tilted
Toward a grey prison tower in the right-hand third

Of the mid-distance, and their sisters and daughters
Waving at them, shouting down, in that way
Painters give paint sound and temperature,
Musicians give music colour, the prisoners in the grey
Tower giving their people their need for clothes
And stories, even as one woman in the audience
Turns away. In the museum in Galway you can't
Hear anything they say. The wind filled my ears.
I felt vertigo for the first time, as if I'd slammed into
The back of myself, then into the rock. Part of me
Wanted to keep going, to follow the trajectory
Of my feeling as one sentence, one thought,
No matter where it might take me. That night
Annie and I would fuck to the backbeat
Of the wedding band and rain, the voices of friends
Feeling their way to their rooms as if struck blind
By ceremony, the freshly divided light of hotel hallways,
Fuck me, CCTV. But before that we sat in the car
And ate bread and burning cheese from Ennis, read
The Auroras of Autumn, and made plans to join
The N67 to Ballyvaughan and the Burren, with its
Brodie helmets of hills, its rare indigenous orchids,
Its dapple-grey horses nuzzling each other
In their frame of stone fencing along the highway,
Then on to Kinvara, Kilcolgan, the Flaggy Shore,
The N18 to Galway, Clarinbridge, Oranmore.

A Dyer's Garden

Into this window plot I transplant
The dyer's garden you gave me,
A mordant to fix our tint and hue
In the meadow light of my mind:

Bloodroot and Woodruff, Lady's
Bedstraw, Hollyhock, Coreopsis,
Hemp Dogbane and Burdock,
Soapberry, Clematis, Rhubarb.

CRANBERRIES

The fields of the Fraser delta are flooded
With water and cranberries. Religious men
In beards and turbans and black waders
Encircle the red fruit. They are sacristans

Of the season. Meanwhile, the deacons,
In white cowls, oversee the preparation
Of the salmon redds in the Fraser River
And the red salmon and the salmon roe.

DIVIS AND THE BLACK MOUNTAIN,
BELFAST, NORTHERN IRELAND
for Stephanie Harrington

We're not of here and the heathland can't see
Us and our camera beyond the kissing gate
With the bog cotton and heather and yellow
Bog asphodels, with the hare and the rare
Bog-spotted orchid, the wheaters and reed
Buntings, their circuits and transistors
Alerting us to our own presence, the one
Lost whimbrel hopscotched from the Hebrides.
Only the cattle feeding in the mud beneath
The slow dark fleet of clouds track us
Up the sheep path past the badger sett
To the transmitter mast the British pitched
When the only people who shared this view
Shared it through riflescopes, handheld radios.

THE IRISH CLIFFS OF MOHER BY WALLACE STEVENS

At the Cliffs of Moher we sat in the hired car
And I read you "The Irish Cliffs of Moher"
By Wallace Stevens while a barefaced rook
Went jackbooting across the silver hood.
"Who is my father in this world, in this
House,"—line break— "At the spirit's base?"
I read slowly and as if there were no question
Who understood and who was "shadows
Like wind" and who was going "back to a parent
Before thought, before speech," and who
Finally, was queued with the cold buffetings
Of air fleeing the Atlantic, with the despotic
Crow and his skin-helmet and his look,
That weird black bird, "at the head of the past."

CAPTAIN AHAB AND THE GREAT SHROUD OF THE SEA

The body lets no one forget. Even that child
With the cavity going right through her
Tooth to where the roots have not yet formed,
The child who falls now through the dark lake,
Opaque enamel of ice rising above her
And described in the ice a penetrating hole
Of blue light through which no one looks
Because she was just there and now gone,
Through which, after evening is inked,
Portable lights are trained. Even Jeff Buckley
In all his clothes following that speedboat
Down the secret of the Mississippi River
As if it could ever be enough to just disappear
With something as ancient and single-minded
As the Mississippi River, and go wherever it goes,
Full of mud and litter, the bodies of animals,
Abandoned cars, effluent, highway runoff
Emptying into the Gulf of Mexico. Even
The Gulf of Mexico with its deep water
Wells trembling in another ether. Even
The diver with his pneumonic devices,
His flippers and searchlight and neoprene
Descending now through the portal of ice,
Jeff Buckley singing Leonard Cohen in his mind,
And the poor family huddled on the shore
Beneath the willows, breathing out a cosmos
Of water vapour in the cold night, all the absent
Stars overhead like missing teeth in a mouth
Of such expanse that all things exist within it
And are cancelled in one last involuntary breath.

The Dead Know All About Us
for Jocelyne Baker

Then the blue winter light hardened to hoarfrost
On the oat grass and bentop and rye brome
And on the naked apple trees and the apple sheds
With their ripe fragrance of autumn apples
—Honeycrisp, Pink Lady, Cox's Orange Pippin—
And boudoired the Mennonite schoolhouse
In a white lace so ostentatious and sexy she
Awaited shyly her plain and devoted children.
That winter as we ran we spoke less and less
About your dead husband who fell in stride
Beside us through the trees and past the horse pastures
And the farmhouses and the empty orchards.
Between the logs of the log home he built
For you he laid lambswool to keep out the cold.

THE *ILIAD*, OR THE POEM OF FORCE BY SIMONE WEIL

Someone was there and, the next moment, no one.
I've been reading *The Iliad* for years. The bath
Andromache warmed for her husband is cold now.
But Hector, alone beyond the city walls, was not
Too far from warm baths. He was
The two hundred-fourteenth man killed in *The Iliad*.

FROM TREATY 6, FORT CARLTON, FORT PITT, AND BATTLE RIVER, 1876

After the buffalo were disappeared, by treaty,
The Cree were guaranteed *four hoes for every family*
Actually cultivating; also, two spades per family:
One plough for every three families and one harrow;

Two scythes and one whetstone, and two hay forks
And two reaping hooks, for every family, and also
Two axes; and also one cross-cut saw, one hand-saw,
one pit-saw, the necessary files, one grindstone

And one auger for each Band; and also for each Chief
For the use of his Band, one chest of ordinary
Carpenter's tools; also, for each Band, enough of
Wheat, barley, potatoes and oats to plant the land

Actually broken up for cultivation by such Band;
Also for each Band four oxen, one bull and six cows;
Also, one boar and two sows, and one hand-mill
When any Band shall raise sufficient grain therefor.

LA BAUME BONNE
Musée de Préhistoire des gorges du Verdon

The good cave. Tucked up in the cliffs of Verdon,
Prehistory, where-we-come-from. That's you
Shucking snails with a stick. That's me learning
To hide under a hide, naked. The progressive

Abandonment of relative chronologies. The slow
Sedimentary drip of turquoise minerals, ancestry.
Thus each excavation phase is a reflection
Of an idea of an idea. We see it mocked-

Up in the Musée—on film and 3D—our heads
Gripped by black omegas that speak to us
Our language, the current last words on how
We imagine we imagine what it was like

Before cooking fires, stone knapping, the Levallois
Technique. And after. All that absence in absence
In absence. The good cavity. We've been
Coming here as a family year after year after year.

Knowth, Brú na Bóinne, Co. Meath, Ireland

My grief is no more grief with money.
No less. The American on the bus
To Knowth is all presence. I'm trying
To picture life in this townland along
The River Boyne before the fields
Were trenched and quicked with thorn,
Hedgerows, property, wealth. Before
Acts of Parliament. William of Orange.
At Clogherhead, the masons carved
The impossible granite, lifetime after
Lifetime, and guided the slabs by sea
To the riverhead. There was no hope
They'd see the passage grave complete, lit
Only by the light of our most even days.

Music Lesson

All the children of Bevan crowd around
To study the xylophone of vertebrae
The deer has left on the schoolhouse floor.
It is so serious in the abandoned school

We can hear the fiddleheads perform.
Ever-so-slowly, the students pair off
And dance a reel over the broken floor
And the tree roots and between the trees.

OKANAGAN GNEISS

I was doing something wrong with my life.
In the highlands, sunlight outlined the lodgepole pine
Making a black absence in the blue sky
The exact shape of a pine. Let me sketch for you
The red cedar alone in the lower dark
With its sash of moss woven from pure-green
Filaments of age, or the white aspen swimming
In its riffle of sky, or the vine maple's
Old Welsh scrawled in gnarled script
Across the underbrush. Yes, I was doing something wrong
With my life. Listen. The foley has forgotten
The birdcall and your stomach and the horse's
Breath but not the brittle tick of leaves
Falling like sunlight, like someone approaching fast from behind.
Everything we need to know is locked up
In this folio of rock I see you reading with your mind.
Nothing is too hard when you know how alone you are.

I Don't Want to Die Like Frank O'Hara

Because Frank O'Hara talked to the sun he had to die
On Fire Island. "Maybe we'll speak in Africa,"
The sun said, "of which I too am specially fond."
"Don't go," O'Hara said but the sun was already
A big wheel of fire over the East African Plateau
And the plantations of aloe vera and the boy
With the Kalashnikov nuzzled against his skull.
"They are calling," the sun said before whispering
Something about a poem. "Who are they?" O'Hara
Wanted to know, but the boy held a paring knife
And, using his left hand to guide, carefully cut
The lips from a husband and his wife. "Some day
You'll know," the sun told him. "They are calling
To you too." I don't want to die like that boy
Didn't want to die and O'Hara didn't want to die
In 1966 on Fire Island. "Darkly he rose," O'Hara says
Of the sun and the Kalashnikov and the child
In the field of aloe who did what he did for no reason
Except he didn't want to die. "Go back to sleep,
Frank," the sun said. Darkly he rose and the poet slept.

Bring Me the Head of Emiliano Zapata Salazar

When Zapata's followers wished to salute him as Generalissimo,
He replied, "Emiliano Zapata is dead." In all of Morelos,
Between the upland pastures and the hot lowlands,
The countryside settled its own questions. In the plaza
The band played "La Paloma" and the priests fled
Across the border in advance of the last dollar. So, quaintly,
The churches were turned into motion picture houses,
Schools, and poultry exhibitions. The country teemed
With waggish song. Every woman was as wealthy
As every man and there was not a single coin
Or bill of money. The pay was the freedom of the union
From cabbage basket to opera house. Each member
Of the community wore about his neck a disc of brass.
On it was inscribed: "One hundred years ago, a humble priest
Named Morelos kept in the field a revolutionary army."
With the disc the Indian could present himself on a train
Or put up at a hotel without price. There could be no haggling.

1977

Maria Callas is dead and Groucho Marx.
Loren Eiseley is dead. Vladimir Nabokov
And Robert Lowell and Elvis. Dead.
This is the year in the Years of Lead
When the Metropolitan Indians rioted
In Bologna after the carabinieri shot
Francesco Lorusso. They wore war paint
And skittered and gagged at the tanks
While Johnny Lyndon celebrated the Queen's
Jubilee on a boat out on the Thames,
Eighty-seven years after Wounded Knee.
This is the year the States reinstated
The death penalty and Gary Gilmore
Gave his final grin at 8:07 a.m. in front
Of a firing squad at Utah State Prison.
Charlie Chaplin, dear friends, is dead.
The public intellect is looking for a body
In a garage in Los Altos, Silicon Valley.
This is the year of the ersatz investment
In irony, competition, the comedic value
Of total violence we recognize finally
As the final admonishment of the modern.
A year of 3.3 million human zygotes
Soaking in the sodium light of imagination.
The sun is booming. Emanuel Jaques
Drowns in a sink at 245 Yonge Street
And Gerald Hannon publishes "Men Loving
Boys Loving Men" in *The Body Politic*.
The humours are comely and bilious.
I'm not alive to laugh about any of this.

THE ASSASSINATION OF ACHILLES THE CRUEL

After the horses watered at the tomb of Ilus,
Hermes, child star, quisling, junior bagman
For the family business, breathed his boozy nothings
In the team's twitchy, whisky-coloured ears
And bitter Priam, his chariot loaded to the tits
—Twelve cloaks, brocades, the Thracian cup,
The year's picks in white capes and robes,
Four fine cauldrons, ten perfect bars of gold—
Went careening across the blood-skunked plains
To the trench and rampart around the fleet
Where the Achaean sentries had just set down
For supper and seeing the hillbilly king
With his kit and caboodle of guilt and grief
Felt kerschnickered and conked out in their grub.
In the great pine lodge beyond the courtyard,
Beneath a thatch of meadow reeds, no one noticed
Priam park his battle-car pimped with payola
And dipsy-doodle, the spry beggar, through
Feast tables filled with captains of the fleet
Who would have choked in horror and disbelief
Had they peeped the beleaguered king,
Down on his knee, get the jump on Achilles.

DOVE CREEK HALL (FORMERLY SWEDES' HALL)

The children play their fiddles so slowly I am sad
For the old wooden hall among the cow patties.
Who cut the rhodo blooms and set them on the piano?
They bow tiredly through every tune. Even the cows
Have wandered away from the music to the far side
Of the pasture. All the Swedes who built this hall
Are dead now and the women they married are dead
And the pastor who married them and their friends.
But the children do not know this or just how sad
Beauty is on the last day of spring with instruments
And young players making music beneath the rafters.
They play along with mistakes and embarrassment.
Tell me, who hung the hand-stitched stars on the wall?
Who hung the evening light from the windows?

for Grant Shilling

Everywhere I go I bring myself and I'm lonely.
It's 1773. Eileen O'Connell keens for Art O'Leary
On a horse across seven miles of County Cork.
"I'm a relic from a time that never was,"
My friend laughs in a late episode of dusk.
His father has died and now he says Kaddish
Below the slow dusty mirrorball of the moon.
There are beautiful old women recalling
Themselves in hotel rooms. There's Eileen
O'Connell, who drank of the blood of Art O'Leary
And calls now for him to rise up and pay
For his drinks with his own money. Me again.
"I'm an elegiac person," Larry Levis said before
He died and then again later in all his poems.

FALCON HILL, LOVER'S WALK, CORK CITY, IRELAND
for Jim and Olive Green

In Jim and Olive's garden above the Lee
The eternal yew is never threatened
And the copper beech remembers
The lepers walking the high-walled
Street named for lovers to bathe
Sore and deformed feet in the river.
Sarah Curran may have strolled here
With Robert Emmet the winter before
He was drawn and quartered. This morning,
I feast on rashers and black pudding
And the clocks on the stained glass
Shandon Jim rescued from the Hotel
Maldron tell the same times they always
Tell the roses and the rhododendrons.

From The Lives of North American Horses

✴

There are no more wild horses, the visiting author
says, only feral ones. He's written two books on
thoroughbreds, which are all descended, he tells us,
from the same English mares and Arabian stallions
that King Henry VIII bred. Henry dreamt of a horse
as stable as the mares that bore knights in plated
armour over the soggy fields of northern Europe and
as swift as the stallions that kicked sand across the
orient, that Allah, himself, conjured from the south
wind.

✴

I want to make a creature of you, Allah said.
Condense!

✴

When your kids were small, and from a car window
you spied a horse entertaining a lonely crowd of
pasture, like a fool you shouted *Feral Equus!* and
summoned delight to your daughters' eyes, as if
you'd identified something rare, magical, something
deserving of their breathless attention, something
that exists beyond the ordinary, that barely exists,
a flicker, a vibration, something formed in the
language of the dead.

✴

Nowadays, the author continues, some seventy
per cent of racehorses can claim descent, if claiming
descent were a thing a horse would do, from
Northern Dancer, that most Canadian of racehorses,
who came so close to winning the Triple Crown but
was outlegged at the Belmont Stakes by a stallion
called Quadrangle and a gelding called Roman
Brother.

⤶

Then from the material condensed from the wind—
and you quote—he made a kamayt-coloured animal
(a bay or burnt chestnut) and said, I call you Horse; I
make you Arabian and I give you the chestnut colour
of the ant; I have hung happiness from the forelock
which hangs between your eyes; you shall be the
Lord of the other animals. Men shall follow you
wherever you go; you shall be as good for flight as
for pursuit; you shall fly without wings; riches shall
be on your back and fortune shall come through
your meditation.

⤶

In the early days the Latin drove your six-year-older daughter crazy. The elevated diction felt both too scientific and too regal for these large hairy animals chewing grass in the Pacific rain. The words did not fit what she understood to be the conditions of the world: the horses were horses, not subjects of investigation or rule, and the pasture was a pasture, not a grassland, not a prairie, not something that had escaped or been abandoned by domesticity, by the order of human beings.

⊥

Who is the monarch but the arbiter of truth? What is science but the ruler, the measure, of reality?

⊥

Thus speaks Kikkuli, master horse trainer of the land of Mitanni. And thus begins the oldest surviving manual on horse training in the known world. Written in the Hittite language, it is important for both what it says about horses and about the development of Indo-European languages. Kikkuli, it seems, had difficulty finding the words so that others might understand what he understood about horses.

⊥

In those years, you saw horses daily as you drove the country roads to your daughters' school. Now, living in a different part of the world, attending different schools, seeing horses only occasionally when you drive out into the hills surrounding your small Canadian city, your children still children, but older, more separate, already travelling on their own, you play the game, say the words, out of habit, memory, the residue of a charge trapped in another time, another geography.

⤶

You were born in the Chinese Year of the Horse, long after the coming of the Sea Peoples to the Levant but before the Seven Days War.

⤶

On Sunday, driving past a black mare hanging her head over the wooden beams of a fence, the Latin felt almost bitter—almost because it was not as galvanizing as bitterness. The absurdity had been displaced from language onto something even more conditional—as in a function of conditions—which are not ironic or reflected but experienced, lived, in the first degree.

⤶

I am a Hittite in love with a horse, says Frank
O'Hara in memory of his feelings.

⤋

Walking the dirt road between the small pastures
and the flooded salt flat, the late February sun
shaving the membrane of ice on the shallow lake,
your friend Mary and you see a tawny horse with
shaggy tassels on its leg above the fetlocks. The
horse is tipped on its side so its white belly faces the
road. A ditch filled with water and reeds separates
the animal from you, you from the animal. And
a wooden fence. No real barriers to a moderately
determined human or a moderately wild horse. Your
first thought and Mary's: the horse is dead.

⤋

The horse as we know it evolved in North America.
More than two million years ago, wild horses from
this continent crossed the Bering land bridge and
populated Asia. In those days, all animals were wild.
The children can't stop laughing.

⤋

Let's do some living after we die, Mick Jagger says in
a song about horses.

⤋

It's 1956. Edwin Muir publishes the most anthologized poem of his career. Called "The Horses," the poem depicts the return of wild horses to a world plunged into a pre-industrial state as the result of an unspecified global horror known as the Seven Days War. Return is met with return. Edwin Muir is perhaps best remembered, along with his wife, Willa Anderson, as our most highly regarded translator into English of the works of Franz Kafka. Late in the summer, Muir writes, the strange horses came. Our life is changed.

⤙

It is generally agreed that near the end of the last ice age the indigenous horses of North America disappeared from the continent. This was only 10,000 years ago, a time that saw the arrival of more humans to the continent though it is not clear what role humans had in the extinction. Some evidence exists that wild horses may have persisted even longer, maybe another 5 or 6,000 years, bringing them tantalizingly close to the active memory of the indigenous peoples of these lands, the lands where you now live.

⤙

Your ex-wife's father—your daughters' grandfather—
was called John but also Crazy Horse and sometimes
just Horse. These latter two names, one or the other,
is written in ballpoint pen across the sleeves of all the
vinyl records your ex-wife inherited from him after
he died—five crates, including *Sticky Fingers* by the
Rolling Stones, an album most famous for the song
"Wild Horses." John died of a heroin overdose in
1995. You and he never met and he never met your
children. Heroin is a drug sometimes called *horse*.

⤙

When the horse lifts its head to look at you and your
friend, out there between the pasture and the salt
flat—the alkaline playa—you are both appalled by
your lack of manners. Don't get up, you say. It's a
myth that horses only sleep standing up. We know
that. Enjoy the sun. Put down your head.

⤙

Columbus carried no horses in 1492, but in 1493
he set sail with twenty fighting horses and five
dobladuras from Granada.

⤙

Your children pedal their bikes for hours through
the suburbs.

⤙

In one of Elizabeth Bishop's ballads a grandfather and granddaughter ride in a wagon. When they get to Hustler Hill the grandfather announces the mare is tired. They get down and walk as good manners require.

via iMessage

Mary
Wtf. I thought you were my ally in ██████████
████.

Matt
What am I supposed to do? I'm ███████.

Mary
I know. I'm concerned I have hitched my wagon to the wrong horse.

Matt
███

Mary
I guess I don't really care. You're the only horse I'm interested in.

Mary
In . . . a non-weird way. Please read that non-weirdly.

Matt
Ha! Don't get up . . . we know you're not dead . . .

Mary
. . . yet . . .

↓

On a different Sunday in May, Annie and you drive
into the port town of Clifden, in the Connemara
region of Co. Galway. The sun has come out, and
miraculously the streets are full of horses and
riders. Later you learn it is a famous pony market
that attracts horse traders from across Ireland and
Europe. Later still you spend several hours online
reading the names and pedigrees of the ponies
that had been for sale that day in Clifden, on the
Owenglen River, where, in 1905, Guglielmo Marconi
built his first long-wave wireless telegraph station, a
site he chose specifically to minimize the distance
to its sister station on the eastern coast of North
America.

↓

Let the dark skies open on the blurry animals. Let
the blanket girls cross the sea of time to cover their
cold withers.

↓

It's 1519. The Spanish Conquistador, Hernán Cortés, begins his march through the breadnut and sapodilla across the Plains of Mexico. In Veracruz he asks the tributaries of the Aztecs for a meeting with Moctezuma II, the ruler of the Aztec Empire, who lives in a palace on an island in Lake Texcoco. Moctezuma refuses. With Cortés in Veracruz are over 700 soldiers, 15 cannons, and 16 horses. According to Spanish reports, the natives have never seen horses and believe horse and rider are one animal.

⤙

Franz Kafka's most famous story is one of a man turned into a beast. When he died he left an unfinished novel called *Amerika*.

⤙

Moctezuma dreams of his mother, who, in the dream, has her own dream of her mother's mother's mother. In that dream within a dream Moctezuma's distant grandmother is telling a story of an animal that can run for days and days and one day runs so far it disappears and is never seen again. When he awakes sunlight bathes his face and the unknown stench of horses occupies his nostrils.

⤙

A horse that has never won a race is called a maiden. A horse that gives up mid-race or otherwise quits before finishing is said to have puked. You learn these terms from the visiting author who before thinking about racehorses worked on a book about two trips the Canadian rock legend Neil Young made across the continent in a hearse in the late 1960s. In 1975, four years after the Stones' *Sticky Fingers*, Young released the song "Cortez the Killer," which is either about Hernán Cortés, or the dissolution of Young's relationship to Carrie Snodgrass, or both. The song was recorded with his long-time band, Crazy Horse.

⤙

How long must something go feral before it becomes wild again?

⤙

You once believed your father was Neil Young. Or rather, the man in denim walking down a country road on the album cover of *Old Ways* looked to you like your dad wearing denim and walking down a country road in what you might have called real life. For *real life*, your youngest daughter sometimes says when she wants to clarify what is directly true from what is only indirectly true. Some years ago you wrote a poem that re-imagines a story you'd been told about your father. The poem is about being lost in middle age. It is also about friendship and truth, both the direct and indirect varieties. The poem ends with the image of two horses in a winter field. The horses represent your father and his friend from the story. They also represent you, as you are today in middle age, and your father, when he was even younger.

                    ⅄

According to Bernal Díaz del Castillo, who recorded the 1519 expedition to Lake Texcoco, among the horses with Cortés was a vicious dark chestnut that died when they arrived at San Juan de Ulúa; a very good sorrel mare; a grey mare called La Robana; a good grey mare charger; four dark chestnuts; a patched sorrel not good for warfare; a dapple horse with stockings on the forefeet; another dapple horse that was almost black; a light chestnut; a good dark horse called El Arriero—a kind of meta-nickname meaning "the horsemen"—and a chestnut mare that had foaled on the ship. There is no mention of the foal in Castillo's account.

                    ⅄

Every year, in the first part of July, the Travellers—a long-mistrusted, indigenous Irish minority known for their traditionally nomadic lifestyle—attend the Cahirmee Horse Fair in Buttervant, County Cork, to trade horses and arrange marriages. Their history as breeders of the finest horses in Ireland is as integral to their identity as their songs and caravans, as their giant, carnivalesque weddings, as their shunning. You learned this from a special series on National Public Radio called "The Hidden World of Girls," in which the voices of several Traveller women can be heard telling of their weddings at 13, 15, 16 years of age. Traveller girls don't mix much with settled girls, one of the voices says, and you imagine your settled girls unsettled in shotgun orange skirts and shotgun orange tops—as the girl from Monaghan describes her friend's outfit—wearing crowns and riding toward marriage on the biggest wagon pulled by the most beautiful blue horse. Cahirmee was a meeting point, the radio program explains, for a people who were rooted, but rarely still, and a wedding was a chance for a girl to escape control of her father.

⤋

The historical Crazy Horse, the man who fought
like a wild person at the Battle of Little Big Horn,
was born between 1840 and 1845 in a year that
the Lakota are said to have stolen over 100 horses
during their winter count. He was the third man in
his family to be called Crazy Horse. He died under
suspicious circumstances while in the custody of the
United States of America. According to Black Elk,
Crazy Horse was never known to dance or sing, but
in a vision, where the trees and stones and grass had
all become spirit, he met his own horse standing still
among the celestial chaos. Then the horse began to
dance like an animal made only of shadow.

⤜

You only now mention the famous Trojan Horse,
that giant wooden superstructure that was received
inside the walls of Troy as a gift and that carried
within it a secret that would destroy everything:
inside such acts of civilization hides the memory of,
and impulse to, wilderness, to violence. Who is more
feral than the soldier in the theatre of war? Who is
more undone than the child wielding language?

⤜

From that destruction of Troy came the founding
of a new Troy. From the new Troy came the word
Equus: Northern Dancer. Quadrangle. Roman
Brother. Condense!

↓

Three names from the Clifden pony registry:
Owens Eagle, Outta Touch, Young Grace.

↓

As of 2010 there were some 33,700 mustangs, or feral
horses, in the mountains and grasslands of North
America.

↓

Coda: Eyesight

Once, for a time, I lost my sight. It was winter
        solstice
    when day is only a thin slot

Between darknesses. In the forge of my eyes
        a virus
    the colour of dimes

began to counterfeit itself and circulate
        in the pockets
            of newly minted retinal cells.

    So

            in the field
of my vision appeared
                grey stipples of dim translucence

as if the winter sky had drifted between me
        and the world.

First the lamp in the corner of

        the room disappeared

            then the corona of lamplight
on the bare wall

then the shadow of that light—

Is the lamp better off, Seneca asks, before it's lit
        or after
                it's put out?

        But he's not really asking.
Anything is enough when you know how poor you are.
        That's Levis.

All I ever wanted to know
                        is how to be

at home
        with myself.

Later, when the lamp reappeared it was only a lamp

        without the corona of light
                or the shadow of that light

        or the room. Inside the lamp
I could see

                        nothing

        but a soft glow.

NOTES

The epigraph from Gwendolyn Brooks comes from her poem "Boy Breaking Glass."

The Frank O'Hara epigraph is from his poem "In Memory of My Feelings."

"Winter Horses" adapts a line from Michael Longley's poem "A Norwegian Wedding."

"Mavis Gallant" paraphrases John Berryman's poem "Dream Song 14." The phrase "loneliness is solitude with a problem" belongs to Maggie Nelson, from her collection *Bluets*.

"Talking Trojan War Blues" quotes and misquotes Robert Hass's poem "Meditation at Lagunitas."

"The Irish Cliffs of Moher by Wallace Stevens" quotes directly from "The Irish Cliffs of Moher" by Wallace Stevens.

"Captain Ahab and the Great Shroud of the Sea" borrows a phrase—"trembling in another ether"—from Wallace Stevens's "Esthétique du Mal." The title borrows from a phrase at the end of Herman Melville's *Moby-Dick*.

"Music Lesson" refers to the Vancouver Island ghost town of Bevan.

"I Don't Want to Die Like Frank O'Hara" quotes directly from "A True Account of Talking to the Sun on Fire Island" by Frank O'Hara.

The text of "Bring Me the Head of Emiliano Zapata Salazar" is a cut-up of a *One Big Union Bulletin* from October 1919 that was reprinted in a Red Lion Press pamphlet.

"1977" borrows details from Franco "Bifo" Berardi's text *The Uprising: On Poetry and Finance*.

"Alice Munro" borrows a line I (mis)remember from an interview with Larry Levis. It also makes reference to "The Lament for Art O'Leary," a famous keen I know best in translation by Vona Groarke.

"Falcon Hill, Lover's Walk, Cork City, Ireland" refers to the Shandon bell tower, famous for its four clocks, each of which tells a different time. The tower is locally referred to as "The Four-Faced Liar."

ACKNOWLEDGEMENTS

Versions of many poems previously appeared in *All Hollow* (ro/us), *Arc, Best American Poetry Blog, Best Canadian Poetry 2015, B O D Y* (cz), *Carousel, Event, The Fiddlehead, Hazlitt* (online), *The Lonely Crowd* (uk), *The Malahat Review, Prism International, Riddle Fence, The Rusty Toque, Shining Like an Apple on Fire, 32 Poems* (us), *Tag,* and *The Walrus.* My sincere gratitude to the publishers, curators, and custodians of each of these venues: you are the first folk who tend and attend to the public life of our language.

Versions of some of these poems were previously collected in the chapbook *I Don't Want to Die Like Frank O'Hara* from Baseline Press. Great thanks to Karen Schindler.

This book was written with assistance from the Canada Council for the Arts and the British Columbia Arts Council. Thank you to the University of British Columbia Okanagan, the Faculty of Creative and Critical Studies, and the Office of Research Services for the privilege of your ongoing support of my creative work.

A very special thank you to the poet John Ennis, who first invited me to Ireland, welcomed me, fed me, introduced me to his people, and gave me a place to be with myself for a time.

To all the people at McClelland & Stewart, thank you for giving this book a life.

To my editor, Ken Babstock, a profound respect for helping me find a clearer version of my poems.

To all the friends, past and present, who read drafts at various points over the years and who offered criticisms and encouragements: your voices are whispering in the ear of each of these poems. A particular thank you to my dear friends Chris Hutchinson and Michael V. Smith for the light of their minds on this manuscript.

To my family.

To my daughters, Neela and Nora.

Thank you.

Unspeakable Acts in Cars

It's the first day of summer and we're so happy
To see the sun and the satchel of colours it schleps
All those dark kilometres. The sky is so blue
And the sea is blue and the small islands in the sea
Are blue also. How our sun must love blue.
We have beachgrass and bull kelp and lion's mane
And we love them all because we love the sea
Which is cold and buoyant. Friends now of sea salt
And knotweed, the mountains know all about us
And who we are when we are most ourselves.
But their blue haughty distances are no help.
We are who we are with mock orange and wisteria.
We've nothing to bitch about. The high cirrus
Can't touch us. We been alive just long enough.

.